ALLEN PHOTOGR

C000055410

ALL ABOUT
BEDS AND BEDDING

CONTENTS

BEDDING DECISIONS

Deciding which bedding to use for your horse is no longer a simple choice between straw and shavings. The bedding market has become so advanced that now you can choose a bedding that is tailored to suit your horse's every need, just as you would choose a mattress to suit yourself.

With so many alternatives on the market, it is difficult to decide which bedding material and management routine will fulfil your own needs, without unnecessary expense. Are you satisfied with your existing bedding system, or do you feel you are spending unnecessary time and money in maintaining your horse's stable?

Remember that the less time your horse spends in the stable, the less time and money you will spend on maintaining the bed and the happier the horse will be. If the horse does not soil the bed excessively, highly absorbent materials are an unnecessary expense and standard bedding will suffice.

STORAGE

Do you have limited storage for bedding materials? Paper, woodshavings and most of the straw alternatives are compact and wrapped in a waterproof covering for easy outdoor storage. If you use standard straw, you will need a sufficiently large covered area to keep the straw dry. Remember that during the winter you will have hay to store as well. The ultimate space-saver is rubber flooring, which requires no storage at all.

ANALYSE YOUR NEEDS

Before you get confused, write down the specific requirements for you and your horse. Think about whether these are essential needs or simply what you would like if finances allow.

COSTS TO CONSIDER

Many developments initially seem like a clever way of making horse ownership more expensive. Analyse the benefits, such as increased absorbency or a bitter taste, and you may find that the new bedding lasts longer and actually saves money in the long term. Calculate how much it will cost to fill the stable with each type of bedding and then how much you will need to maintain the bed. Many alternatives to straw and woodshavings are more expensive per bale, but you may need fewer to fill and maintain the bed.

VAT AND DELIVERY

Check whether the quote you are given includes VAT and delivery. Many companies will only offer free delivery for large quantities, so buy in bulk with friends.

When comparing the cost of filling and maintaining the stable with different types of bedding, remember that the volume of bales can vary greatly, depending on the company. Most manufacturers will quote the approximate volume of each bale and offer an estimate of the amount you will need to fill and maintain the average-sized stable.

DEPTH OF BEDDING

If the horse spends a lot of time in the stable, you will need to choose bedding that is highly absorbent. Combine this, if possible, with a deep-litter system that will cushion the horse's legs.

The bed should ideally be between 15 cm (6 in) and 30 cm (12 in) deep.

BANKS

High banks stacked against the wall will reduce draughts, add warmth and protect your horse against injury.

The banks should be at least 30 cm (12 in) deep to minimise draughts and prevent the horse from becoming cast.

If the stable is in a particularly exposed area, or is cold itself, the banks will need to be higher. You may need extra bedding to maintain this system, but you will save money by preventing illness and making your horse more comfortable in the stable. A shallow bed is false economy. Think about how you feel after a bad night's sleep, you certainly are not at your best and it is the same for your horse.

DEEP LITTER

If you need to save time during the week, consider a deep-litter system. This minimises the problems found when the bed is taken up, such as injuries inflicted if the horse tries to lie down or slips on an unprotected surface. Horses are also discouraged from staling if there is no bedding on the floor.

A deep-litter system will enable your horse to lie down in comfort, resulting in a happier and more relaxed horse. This system is unsuitable for horses with respiratory problems as the bed will be difficult to keep dry and potentially high levels of ammonia will irritate the respiratory tract.

If you decide to use this system, think carefully about which bedding to use. If the material has poor levels of absorbency, it will be heavy and unpleasant to muck out by the weekend. This should be considered if you have a large number of horses to manage. Follow the general principle that the more absorbent the bedding is, the more suited it will be to a deep-litter system. Semideep-litter beds are an ideal compromise.

RUBBER SOLUTION

For a horse that has a respiratory problem and is therefore not suited to a deep-litter system, yet has to be stabled for most of the time, rubber flooring will provide the ideal solution (see page 10).

MINIMISE ODOUR

If you find your stable smells strongly of urine, even when you muck out regularly, try using a product designed to prevent the formation of ammonia and hydrogen sulphide in the bedding. This will help you to cut down on the amount of bedding used. Some offer the added advantage of improving the fertilisation value of waste bedding.

BED EATING

Some horses have an annoy-ing tendency to eat their straw bedding instead of the expensive coarse mix you carefully selected, resulting in weight gain, poor perfor-mance and the additional expense of replacing the bedding.

Consider using a specially treated material with an unpleasant, bitter taste to discourage horses from eat-ing it.

Bed eating usually stems from boredom, so one way of reducing this is to keep the horse entertained. The most obvious answer is to turn the horse out as often as circumstances allow. If this is not possible, there are many 'toys' on the mar-ket, such as the Equiball, designed to keep the horse occupied in the stable. Dr Natalie Warren researched the Equiball during her study of stable vices at Edinburgh University.

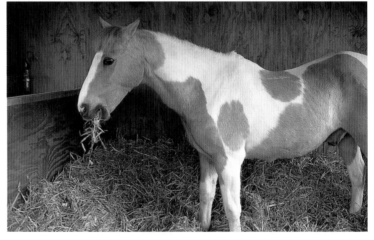

RESPIRATORY PROBLEMS

Chronic Obstructive Pulmonary Disease (COPD) is an allergy to mould spores in straw and hay, therefore a horse stabled on straw cannot escape from the microscopic particles that enter his lungs every time he breathes. If the damage is not prevented, the horse will be left unable to breathe without a struggle.

As well as feeding soaked or vacuum-packed hay, avoid using straw bedding, unless it has been specially treated. Traditional straw beds are notoriously dusty and horses that are prone to respiratory problems would be better suited to dust-extracted bedding. Look for products which are also treated with a non-toxic disinfectant for additional hygiene.

When choosing a management routine for a horse with respiratory problems, it is best to avoid a deep-litter system, to ensure the bed is kept very dry. You may not have to take the bed up daily; try a semideep-litter system where the damp bedding is removed two or three times a week. A damp environment will provide the ideal growing conditions for spore-producing moulds.

SPECIAL TREATMENT!

Some manufacturers pretreat the bedding with a natural pulmonary antiseptic to improve the horse's respiratory capacity and stimulate the vascular system.

MOVING HOUSE!

If the horse is stabled in the same building as other horses bedded on straw, it will be impossible to create a spore- and dust-free environment. If the horse continues to suffer from respiratory problems, alternative stabling should be sought.

TRADITIONAL STRAW

Standard straw is the cheapest and most traditional form of bedding, providing a cosy appearance and a warm, solid bed. It is particularly economical when used in a deep-litter system but, be warned, straw lacks absorbency and is heavy and unpleasant to muck out.

WHAT KIND OF STRAW?

Barley straw is the most suitable type, although it looks appetising to the horse and can lead to bed-eating. Oat straw is more expensive and very palatable, so you may find the horse has eaten the bed before he has a chance to lie on it. This can lead to allergic coughing, made worse by the high dust content.

If you want to use straw, try one of the alternatives on the market. These are usually made from dust-extracted chopped wheat or flax straw, with a bitter taste to discourage bed-eating. They are more efficient and lightweight than long straw and compact easily for rapid disposal, making them ideal for a time-saving deep-litter system. Some alternatives are treated with a nontoxic disinfectant to control bacteria and fungal growth and even repel flies.

SWEET SCENTS

You may find your clothes smell more un-pleasant after mucking out straw beds than others, such as woodshavings. Look for 'fresh scented' and sanitised versions to avoid this.

TREAT IT YOURSELF

Make standard straw unpalatable by spraying it with a nontoxic disinfectant using a garden pump-spray. A solution of diluted tea-tree oil will also keep flies out of the stable during the summer.

FLAX STRAW

This is a dust-free bedding suitable for a deep-litter system, providing a firm, dense, natural bed, which composts quicker than hemp or other wood-based products and is ideal for horses with respiratory problems.

WOODSHAVINGS

Woodshavings are the most common alternative to straw as they are lighter and more absorbent. They are, therefore, ideal for a deep-litter system and reduce the need for additional drainage on an uneven stable floor.

You will find it easier to keep the horse clean on this bedding, but the fine particles make it unsuitable for horses with open wounds. Check the woodshavings for sharp particles that will irritate the horse's skin.

BAG YOUR OWN

You can save money by befriending your local lumberjack! Most sawmills will provide a free supply of woodshavings, although you may have to bag your own. Be aware that the quality of the woodshavings is not guaranteed; look out for sharp pieces of wood, foreign objects and a high dust content.

DUST-EXTRACTED WOODSHAVINGS

If the horse is prone to respiratory problems, be aware that although less dusty than straw, standard woodshavings are not necessarily dust free. Choose dust-extracted versions to be sure of a spore-free environment.

RUBBER FLOORING

A rubber floor will save time mucking out during the week, and will reduce the need for that dreaded week-end clean out. You will be left with manure that is free from bedding, making it ideal to sell to gardeners, who will appreciate a garden free from straw! It is also ideal for field shelters, where any other form of bedding might blow away.

Do not be deterred by the uncomfortable appearance and initial expense of rubber flooring. Many brands offer thermal insulation, so you need not worry about your horse being cold and not having to purchase bedding will even out the cost over time. Horses standing in the stable for long periods will benefit from rubber's cushioning properties. A small patch of bedding will encourage the horse to stale and will then soak up the urine, while keeping the muck heap to a minimum.

Check that the rubber floor has been designed for use without a full bed. Some manufacturers provide surfaces that prevent injury and provide cushioning but are not sufficiently absorbent to use without bedding.

PROTECTION

Fitting wall mats around the base of the stable will increase protection. The mats are ideal for mares in foal and horses requiring a safe, hygienic environment.

WHAT DOES THE PRICE INCLUDE?

There may be hidden costs involved in making the base of the stable and the drainage system suitable for fitting the rubber floor. Consult the manufacturer to find out exactly what installation costs will be involved.

SHREDDED PAPER

This will provide a dust free environment and is ideal for sensitive horses with allergies to straw and spores. However, you may find that the printing ink on paper bedding will irritate horses with white legs.

Shredded paper is absorbent, easy to store outdoors and biodegradable, so it decomposes quickly and is ideal when there is limited space for a muck heap. Bales are wrapped in a waterproof cover but, once opened, you may find the stable and muck heap difficult to keep tidy in windy conditions. Shredded paper does not look particularly attractive, but you should find the advantages outweigh its lack of aesthetic appeal.

OTHER BEDDING MATERIALS

HEMP

This is a natural material providing a completely legal alternative to straw! It has particularly absorbent qualities, decomposes quickly and is easy to maintain in a deep-litter system.

TREE FIBRE

This has similar qualities to the hemp plant. It provides an absorbent, biodegradable material that reduces odours and breaks down quickly. It is ideal for a semideep-litter system.

PEAT MOSS

This is the least suitable form of bedding for the horse and is infrequently used today. It does prevent spore allergies and bed eating and will rot down on the garden. However, it is difficult to maintain a clean bed as the soiled areas are less visible than on paler coloured bedding, resulting in frequent staining of the horse's coat. You may find that peat is dusty when the bed is initially laid down. It is also not environmentally friendly to go on depleting the dwindling peat supplies.

PREPARING THE STABLE

Before introducing a bedding system, examine the standard of the stable. The floor should be easy to clean and free from cracks to prevent urine, spores and bacteria from building up in uneven areas. Wash the floor regularly with a non-toxic disinfectant as an additional precaution. A slight slope of one to two inches towards a drainage channel will keep the stable free from excess urine. If possible, slope the drainage towards the door, to prevent rain from running into the stable and soaking the front of the bed. A brush-finished floor (*top right*) will further aid drainage and provide grip for the horse.

   Insulating the stable roof will increase the surface temperature of the stable to help keep the horse warm and reduce draughts. Ventilation must be provided to remove stale air, odours and spores and to allow the circulation of fresh air.

MINIMISING DUST INHALATION

Try to prepare the bed in advance of the horse coming back to the stable to give dust time to settle. When possible, remove the horse before shaking up the bed to avoid spore inhalation and injury from misplaced tools. If the horse has to stay in the stable, use a headcollar to tie the horse out of the way. In a barn system, avoid creating dust that may travel into other stables.

WATER SPILLAGE

If you find that your horse is constantly knocking the water bucket over and soaking the front of the bed, try fixing a water bucket holder to the stable wall. Alternatively, place the bucket in a thick rubber tyre in the corner of the stable.

AVOID ROT

If the bed is allowed to compact against wooden walls, it will start to heat and may rot the stable. This problem can be avoided by treating the bottom of the stable wall (up to 60 cm [2 ft]) with black bitumen paint.

EQUIPMENT

You will need

1. Four-pronged fork
2. Shavings fork
3. Shovel
4. Hard broom for sweeping the yard
5. Soft broom for removing dust and cobwebs
6. Dustpan and brush for collecting small piles of bedding or feed
7. Skip or laundry basket
8. Strong gloves
9. Sponge for washing windows
10. Chamois leather for drying and polishing windows
11. Water bucket
12. Non-toxic disinfectant
13. Hoover (if possible)
14. Stepladder to reach ceiling.

FORKS AND BROOMS

With the change in consistency and size of bedding particles, it is no longer sufficient to equip your yard with a simple fork, shovel and broom. A four-pronged fork is suitable for both removing and laying the bed. The two-pronged fork is primarily used to break up bales of straw and for airing the bed. They are not suitable for removing soiled bedding as most of it will fall through the prongs.

Save time and money and reduce wastage significantly by using a tool specifically designed to effectively remove droppings and soiled bedding from shavings or short straw. The latest shavings forks are light, virtually unbreakable and have been developed to make mucking out easier (*above right*). They can even be used in the garden!

The size and weight of many stable tools makes them unsuitable for children or small adults. With this in mind, manufacturers have developed mini versions of the standard woodshavings fork with fewer prongs for easier use (*right*). They are also useful for lifting clean bedding from the surface of a straw bed.

Brooms can be heavy and awkward to use, so choose a size you feel comfortable with. You will need a different sized broom for different tasks. A large stiff broom is suitable for sweeping the yard and scrubbing the floor and walls. Smaller, soft brooms are more suited to dusting down the walls and sweeping out the tack and feed rooms.

AVOID WASTE

If you find you waste bedding when mucking out, reassess whether the bedding you are removing really needs throwing out. Shake droppings in a skip or laundry basket to encourage clean bedding to fall back on the floor.

WHEELBARROWS

You will need a strong, durable yet lightweight wheelbarrow to make journeys to the muck heap less difficult, especially in muddy weather. Metal wheelbarrows are heavy and will require at least one coat of rust-resistant paint to see them through the winter.

HANDY HINT

Use thick, waterproof gloves to remove droppings by hand. This will avoid waste and the manure will be free from bedding. The gloves must be washed regularly.

MINIMISE MESS

If you have the problem of more bedding ending up in your car or being blown around the yard when you move it, use a bale tidy. These stylish sacks will enable you to transport and move bales of hay and bedding easily, keeping mess to a minimum.

LIGHTEN THE LOAD

Two-wheeled barrows are more stable, easier to push and less likely to tip over with a heavy load. They may be more expensive than the one-wheeled barrow but they make emptying manure a pleasure!

TIME AND MONEY SAVERS

- Share duties and equipment with friends.
- Buy bedding in bulk with other horse owners.
- Use a glove and laundry basket to remove droppings without waste.
- Use a special fork designed to be efficient, lightweight and strong.
- It is quicker, safer and easier to muck out with the horse out of the stable. Use this time to let the horse eat his feed.
- Move bales of hay and bedding in a wheelbarrow or bale tidy, to avoid mess.
- Remove droppings at least three times a day before they are trodden into the bed.
- Pick the horse's feet out into a skip before leaving the stable.

TIDY TOOLS

Tools are a potential hazard if they are left lying around. Store them tidily in a designated area, preferably under cover.

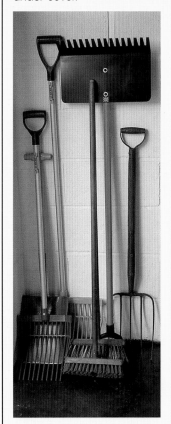

TOOL CARE

All stable tools should be washed at least once a week, preferably with disinfectant, to maintain hygiene and increase their life span. Hang them up to dry then store away safely to avoid rust. Skips and wheelbarrows should be rinsed out daily and allowed to drain.

PREPARING FOR THE NEW BED

When the structure of the stable is warm and safe, you can prepare it for new bedding.

1. Take the horse out of the stable and remove all the old bedding.

2. Hoover or dust the walls, beams, windows, doors and all corners.

3. Wash any fixed surfaces such as hayracks and mangers.

4. Wash the windows and ventilation panels. Check the windows are not loose, cracked or draughty.

5. Wash and scrub the floors with a non-toxic disinfectant. Open the stable door and allow the stable to dry and air thoroughly.

6. The stable is now ready for the new bed to be put down.

MUCKING OUT

DAILY MUCK OUT

Nondeep-litter system Here, the bed is taken up daily, with any soiled bedding being removed. Droppings should be removed throughout the day, as explained for the deep-litter routine.

Semideep-litter system This involves the same daily routine as with deep litter, except that the bed is taken up and the soiled bedding removed two to three times per week instead of just once.

Deep-litter system This system is ideal for busy people who cannot muck out daily but skipping out and freshening the bed should be done as often as possible.

Morning
1. Remove droppings
2. Tidy and reshape the bed.
3. Sweep the stable and yard area.
4. If the horse is out of the stable, open the window and stable door.

Midday
1. Remove any droppings.
2. Sweep if necessary and time allows.

Evening
1. Remove droppings
2. Tidy and reshape the bed.
3. Add fresh bedding if necessary.
4. Sweep the stable and yard area.

Late-night check
1. Remove droppings.
2. Check the horse is secure in the stable and has fresh water for the night.

> **HELPFUL HINT**
>
> If you feed hay from the floor, it is likely to end up scattered around the stable and mixed in with the bedding by the end of the night. Prevent hay being trodden into the bed by feeding from a haynet with small holes or a wall-mounted hayrack.

> **HELPFUL HINT**
>
> Try to disturb the bed as little as possible if the horse has a dust allergy or respiratory problem.

WEEKLY MUCK-OUT

Safety first The horse must be outside the stable in order to complete this job safely and efficiently. Use this opportunity to turn the horse out for some fresh air and exercise.

1. Open windows to minimise the smell and ammonia fumes.

2. Remove any droppings using a skip and glove or a shavings fork.

3. Separate clean bedding with a shavings fork and throw it against the back and sides of the stable. This will also separate small pieces of muck that you may have missed.

4. Using a four-pronged fork, lift the soiled bedding into large sacks.

5. The sacks can then be loaded onto the wheelbarrow or trailer and taken to the muck heap. Putting the soiled bedding into sacks prevents the bedding from being blown around the yard as you take it to the muck heap.

6. Stack the bed at the back of the stable, then sweep the floor to remove all dust.

7. Wash the floor with disinfectant. Look for products designed for equine use. Leave doors and windows open and leave the stable to dry.

8. Once the floor is dry, pull down the remaining bedding so that it covers the floor and provides a solid base for the banks.

9. Add fresh bedding and shape the bed.

10. Sweep the stable and yard area. Once any dust has settled, the horse may be returned to the stable.

DISPOSAL OF BEDDING

If the muck heap has been allotted a small corner of the garden, choose bedding that is lightweight and absorbent so it will compact to a small size and rot quickly. Situate the muck heap where it is usually downwind to minimise mess and odour. Manufacturers will state if their product has been developed for easy disposal. Remember that wood shavings are not easy to dispose of.

THE MUCK HEAP

It will save time and effort if the muck heap is lower than you are when emptying the wheelbarrow. This can be achieved by creating an approach path that is higher than the muck heap. Alternatively, dig a pit in the field into which the soiled bedding can be placed.

If the soiled bedding has to be thrown up, build the muck heap in steps with a flat top surface to allow rain to be absorbed. This will increase the speed of decomposition. Rake the sides to keep them vertical and sweep the area surrounding the muck heap daily. Cover the muck heap with tarpaulin to keep it tidy in windy weather.

BEDDING BREAKDOWN

These materials will decompose quickly:
- Paper
- Short-chopped straw
- Hemp
- Tree fibre
- Flax straw

Arrange for farmers or gardeners to make regular collections from the muck heap. You will find it easier to dispose of bedding in this way if the material decomposes quickly. Paper will break down and be suitable for compost within a few weeks. Putting the soiled bedding directly into a removable skip will make it easier to remove.

PASTURE PROBLEMS

Avoid spreading soiled bedding over pasture used for grazing horses as this will lead to a reduced standard of grass and potential worm infestation. If you have to dump bedding in the field, limit it to a small corner and arrange for frequent removal.

DO NOT BURN BEDDING

Apart from being environmentally unfriendly, burning soiled bedding is against EU regulations. It can also be extremely dangerous if the smoke is likely to blow onto a road.

MAKING A RIDING SURFACE

If you intend to use the soiled bedding to make a riding surface in the field, check that it will not become slippery when wet. Paper bedding is especially poor for this purpose.

HELPFUL HINT

Look out for products designed to promote rapid rotting of soiled bedding. Simply sprinkle it over the muck heap to speed up decomposition, control odour and break down liquid 'run off', making your muck heap more environmentally friendly.

IN CONCLUSION

Remember, although the bedding market is advancing all the time, a conventional straw bed can still provide a comfortable, economical bed for your horse. If you can afford to buy ready treated products, they do have their own advantages but, if money is limited, simply follow the advice in this book to make the most of your standard bedding.

Try not to panic over which bedding and management routine to use. If your horse looks happy and healthy, and is performing to the best of his ability, you have probably got it right!

ACKNOWLEDGEMENTS

Thanks to my beautiful pony Banner for being such a patient and photogenic model – far more so than me! Sadly, since my photos were taken, Banner has passed away at the grand old age of 28. Thanks to my mother and father for their help in setting up the stables, and to my other greatly missed equine companion, Pinky, who inspired me to start writing. Thanks to Dr Natalie Warren from the Institute of Ecology and Resource Management at the University of Edinburgh, for her research on equine stable vices, and finally to the following companies for providing products for photography.

Belvoir Horse Feeds	(Equi-lin/Belvoir Bedding)	Tel: 01522 810741
Davies & Co. Kettering	(Equimat stable flooring)	Tel: 01536 513456
Future Distribution U.K.	(Future Fork)	Tel: 01293 416759
Horsefair	(Le Bedding)	Tel: 01794 389085
Leicester Paper Processors	(Paper Bedding)	Tel: 01530 831355
Rake 'n' Lift & Co	(The Nottingham Tack Rake)	Tel: 0115 9233166
Sinclair Thorman Trading Ltd	(Equiball stable toy)	Tel: 01334 656360
Thermatex	(Chaskit bale bag)	Tel: 01239 614648

(Telephone numbers correct at time of going to print)

British Library Cataloguing-in-Publication Data.
A catalogue record for this book is available from the British Library

ISBN 0.85131.803.7

Published in Great Britain in 2001 by
J. A. Allen an imprint of Robert Hale Ltd.,
Clerkenwell House, 45–47 Clerkenwell Green,
London EC1R 0HT

Design and Typesetting by Paul Saunders
Series editor Jane Lake
Colour processing by Tenon & Polert Colour Processing Ltd., Hong Kong
Printed in Malta by Gutenberg Press Ltd.